ENDORSEMENT

I am so excited about this book taking its place alongside other helpful parenting books. Reading this book will give you a clear step-by-step strategy to engage your teen daughter in a powerful connection with you that enhances her brain development and your impact on her as an individual and possibly a future parent. Janet's writing style is totally nonjudgmental and full of hope—something every parent needs.

— **Cathy Gwin, Psy. D.**

WHAT OTHERS ARE SAYING ABOUT *L.O.V.E.D.*

Sitting down with *L.O.V.E.D.* is like curling up with a cup of coffee and a dear sister you can confide in. Author, Janet Lund, takes what can be an excruciating period for mothers and daughters and gives her readers a simple step-by-step guide on how to cut through the noise and reconnect. Moms who are struggling to communicate with their pre-teen and teenage daughters....and (dare I say it?) older daughters...will find Janet's exercises both engaging and helpful as they reconnect with their daughters!

— **Lori Knutson, Mother and Teacher**

I am a mom to teens. Add in that I'm a publishing professional and entrepreneur and my life is full. It feels as if there is no time in the day to connect with my children. Janet's book took me through easily integrated daily steps to show my kids they are *L.O.V.E.D.* I feel closer to them because of that. I highly recommend you buy this book.

— **Renee Settle, Speaker, Holistic Ghostwriter, 12 Minutes a Day LLC**

I absolutely love *L.O.V.E.D.*! After our son lost his wife to breast cancer, I became GrandMom to their son and daughter. Having raised boys I'm the first to admit I have no clue what to do with this growing girl. Janet's done it again - first with her Mom Keep Calm High Five video series, and now *L.O.V.E.D.* I'm so much more well equipped to navigate these unchartered waters successfully, helping our Gabbie to thrive into adulthood!

> — **Sandy Jones, Publisher,** *Christian Living Magazine*

L.O.V.E.D. offers moms a path to connect with their daughters in a fresh, real way. Drawing on tested strategies and real-life experience, Janet Lund provides wisdom and a hug for moms who want to mend or strengthen their relationship with their daughters.

> — **Stacy Ennis, Author, Speaker, Wife, Mom**

L.O.V.E.D.

*5 SIMPLE STEPS TO CONNECT
WITH YOUR TEEN DAUGHTER*

JANET LUND

For futher information about speaking engagements, professional consultation, special bulk pricing, or other related inquiries, see the author's website at www.momkeepcalm.com.

Cover & Interior Design Concept: Jessica Lund
Cover & Interior Layout: Fusion Creative Works

Print ISBN: 978-0-9889537-7-2

First Printing
Printed in the United States of America

Published by Prepare For Rain Press
A Division of Prepare For Rain LLC
PO Box 171312 | Boise, ID 83717
www.PrepareForRainPress.com

DEDICATION

For my daughter, Jessica

You are my miracle baby,
and you have blessed me from the start.
Hearing your sweet voice sing out, "Momma!"
will forever fill my heart.

❤

Pretty little girl sitting on my back porch.
I'm wonderin' how did we get here?
Cause I swear it was only yesterday,
your voice first rang out in my ear.

Pretty young girl sitting in my driveway,
in my car on the driver's side.
Independence is just round the bend,
so I hide a tear and cheer you on to fly.

— from *How The Years Roll By*, by Janet Lund

Thank you, my precious treasure, for painting my
world in colors beyond my imagination.

ACKNOWLEDGMENTS

Having been a songwriter for many years I knew I had words to share. I just never imagined finding enough words to write a book. But, with some encouragement from my two favorite authors, who are also the loves of my life, they have helped me discover that book writing is like songwriting. When I relax long enough, my thoughts become a meandering pathway through peaceful meadows and friendly forests deep into the backyard of my soul.

Thank you, Kim Foster, for being so supportive of this project. You embraced *L.O.V.E.D.* from the start and cleaned up the bits of feedback that muffled my message.

Thank you, Cathy, for helping me love myself and recognize the ninja in me. You've helped me tackle my feedback loops, so I could hear the words of love from my family clearer than ever before.

Thank you, Jessica, for being my inspiration to want to be the best mom I can be. Until the day I die, I will forever strive to keep growing into the mom you need me to be. P.S. Thank you so much for creating the bear drawings for my book. I love them. They are adorable!

Thank you, Joel, for your unwavering love, support, and your ongoing mission to make me laugh. There are no words to describe how much you mean to me.

I am truly blessed.

Contents

Contents

INTRODUCTION

Hello, Mom!

Welcome to *L.O.V.E.D.* This book was written just for you, Mom. To help you and your daughter connect heart-to-heart once again.

Being a mama bear is a rewarding job but also the most difficult job in the world. This is especially true as your bear cub has nearly matured into a full-grown bear. It is amazing how quickly those little cub years go by, isn't it? One minute she's an infant in your arms; the next she's ready to take on the world.

Now something new is brewing. That lighthearted bear you knew so well does not come out and play as often anymore. Now she is older and moodier. Harder to connect with. Sometimes she even seems aloof.

Growing from childhood into adulthood is a complicated journey. Hormones are kicking in, both her body and brain are changing, and a whole new range of emotions is being discovered. All these changes make it hard for her to feel confident, communicate clearly, and problem-solve. For her it is both scary and overwhelming.

You can't protect your daughter from these changes, but you can support her through them. How? By making her feel completely LOVED!

Of course, loving your daughter has been your mission all along. No question about it! But now it feels like your messages of love no longer reach her heart. The changes that your daughter is going through have an impact on you too, Mom. It can be nerve-rattling at times! Your sweet girl who used to always look up to you now is lashing out at you. This can be hard on your confidence as a parent and as a person.

L.O.V.E.D. will fill your relational toolbelt with the tools you need to (1) replace your feelings of anxious intimidation with calm confidence, (2) nurture a relationship of trust with your daughter, and (3) ensure that your daughter will hear your love for her loud and clear.

I encourage you to take your time. "Marinate" in each chapter. Implement these new skills at your own pace to avoid feeling overwhelmed.

So, are you ready to get started? You go, Mom. You've got this!

Hey, Mama Bear! Hungry for support as you raise your cub through her teen years and beyond? When you finish *L.O.V.E.D.*, please join the *Mom Keep Calm* tribe. You'll discover instructions right after you finish the book. We're here for you.

CHAPTER ONE

L

Welcome to chapter 1 on our mission to help make sure your daughter feels LOVED. To do this we will break this word down letter by letter. First let's focus on the letter L in the word LOVED.

L is for **listen**.

Do you feel like it is always rush hour in your mind? You have millions of things swirling around. Times to remember, schedules to keep track of, deadlines to meet, and expectations to fulfill. You may also have conversations going on inside your head that sound like this:

"How am I going to get this all done?"

"Julie better be ready for me to pick her up, so I can get home and make dinner on time, so I can make my meeting!"

"Did I put last night's load of clothes in the dryer?"

"Where is my phone? I need someone to call me so I can find it. Ahhhhhh!"

Sound familiar?

Before you interact with your daughter, it is important to pause and **listen**. Listen to yourself. Are you chiding yourself? Are you angry at someone else? Are you ready to burst with good news? Whatever conversations are going on in your mind you need to put all of them on a shelf. Quiet yourself down and get prepared to focus on your daughter. It is only by quieting yourself down that you can truly listen to your daughter.

Exercise Part A: 6 Steps to Shelve the Noise

1. Listen to the noise inside your head

2. Become aware of the emotions tied to those thoughts.

3. Be mindful of how those emotions could impact how you react to your daughter.

4. Visualize yourself placing all your thoughts and feelings up on a shelf.

5. Take a few deep breaths: in through your nose, out through your mouth. Take twice as long to blow out as it does to breath it in.

6. Choose to focus on your daughter's heart and listen.

Exercise Part B: Quiet Your Thoughts

Spend time thinking of other ways to quiet your thoughts before engaging in conversation with your daughter. What could you do for yourself? Here are a few suggestions:

- Get a snack and a cup of Joe to fuel up and quiet your hunger pangs.
- Spend 10 minutes reading a page out of a meditation book or devotional.
- Sit in quiet meditation or prayer.
- Visualize getting the outcome you are longing for from your conversation.
- Listen to quiet music to soothe your soul.
- Go for a walk alone to help your whole body relax.

Journaling

Recording your journey is a great way to actively listen to yourself, Mom. Write how breathing and putting your internal noise on a shelf help your conversations with your daughter. Journaling will also help you remember what has been going on in both of your lives. For additional journaling pages go here for a free printable template: bit.ly/LOVED-Journals and put into a 3 ring binder.

Write down your calming ideas:

_____
_____
_____
_____
_____
_____
_____
_____
_____

Write down your self-care plans as you prepare to reconnect with your daughter:

_____
_____
_____
_____
_____
_____
_____
_____
_____
_____
_____

Conversations with my daughter have improved in these ways:

Date:___/___/___ _____

_____

_____

_____

_____

_____

_____

_____

_____

_____

Conversations with my daughter have improved in these ways:

Date:___/___/___ _____

_____

_____

_____

_____

_____

_____

_____

_____

_____

Conversations with my daughter have improved in these ways:

Date:___/___/___ _____

_____

_____

_____

_____

_____

_____

_____

_____

_____

Conversations with my daughter have improved in these ways:

Date:___/___/___ _____

_____

_____

_____

_____

_____

_____

_____

_____

_____

Conversations with my daughter have improved in these ways:

Date:___ /___ /___ _____

_____

_____

_____

_____

_____

_____

_____

_____

_____

Conversations with my daughter have improved in these ways:

Date:___ /___ /___ _____

_____

_____

_____

_____

_____

_____

_____

_____

_____

Conversations with my daughter have improved in these ways:

Date:___/___/___ _____

_____

_____

_____

_____

_____

_____

_____

_____

_____

Conversations with my daughter have improved in these ways:

Date:___/___/___ _____

_____

_____

_____

_____

_____

_____

_____

_____

_____

Conversations with my daughter have improved in these ways:

Date:___/___/___ _____

_____

_____

_____

_____

_____

_____

_____

_____

Conversations with my daughter have improved in these ways:

Date:___/___/___ _____

_____

_____

_____

_____

_____

_____

_____

_____

**Conversations with my daughter have
improved in these ways:**

Date:___ / ___ / ___ _____

_____

_____

_____

_____

_____

_____

_____

_____

_____

**Conversations with my daughter have
improved in these ways:**

Date:___ / ___ / ___ _____

_____

_____

_____

_____

_____

_____

_____

_____

_____

_____

**Conversations with my daughter have
improved in these ways:**

Date:___/___/___ _____
_____
_____
_____
_____
_____
_____
_____
_____
_____

**Conversations with my daughter have
improved in these ways:**

Date:___/___/___ _____
_____
_____
_____
_____
_____
_____
_____
_____
_____
_____

(content)

Conversations with my daughter have improved in these ways:

Date:___/___/___ _____

_____

_____

_____

_____

_____

_____

_____

_____

Conversations with my daughter have improved in these ways:

Date:___/___/___ _____

_____

_____

_____

_____

_____

_____

_____

_____

Conversations with my daughter have improved in these ways:

Date:___ / ___/ ___ _____

_____

_____

_____

_____

_____

_____

_____

Conversations with my daughter have improved in these ways:

Date:___ / ___/ ___ _____

_____

_____

_____

_____

_____

_____

_____

Conversations with my daughter have improved in these ways:

Date:___ /___ /___ _____

_____

_____

_____

_____

_____

_____

_____

_____

Conversations with my daughter have improved in these ways:

Date:___ /___ /___ _____

_____

_____

_____

_____

_____

_____

_____

_____

_____

Conversations with my daughter have improved in these ways:

Date:___ /___ /___ _____

_____

_____

_____

_____

_____

_____

_____

_____

_____

Conversations with my daughter have improved in these ways:

Date:___ /___ /___ _____

_____

_____

_____

_____

_____

_____

_____

_____

_____

_____

**Conversations with my daughter have
improved in these ways:**

Date:___ /___ /___ _____

_____

_____

_____

_____

_____

_____

_____

_____

_____

**Conversations with my daughter have
improved in these ways:**

Date:___ /___ /___ _____

_____

_____

_____

_____

_____

_____

_____

_____

_____

_____

_____

Conversations with my daughter have improved in these ways:

Date:___ /___ /___ _____
_____
_____
_____
_____
_____
_____
_____
_____
_____

Conversations with my daughter have improved in these ways:

Date:___ /___ /___ _____
_____
_____
_____
_____
_____
_____
_____
_____
_____

Conversations with my daughter have improved in these ways:

Date:___/___/___ _____

_____

_____

_____

_____

_____

_____

_____

_____

_____

_____

Conversations with my daughter have improved in these ways:

Date:___/___/___ _____

_____

_____

_____

_____

_____

_____

_____

_____

_____

_____

Conversations with my daughter have improved in these ways:

Date:___ / ___/ ___ _____

_____

_____

_____

_____

_____

_____

_____

_____

_____

_____

Conversations with my daughter have improved in these ways:

Date:___ / ___/ ___ _____

_____

_____

_____

_____

_____

_____

_____

_____

_____

_____

_____

Conversations with my daughter have improved in these ways:

Date:___ / ___ / ___ _____

_____
_____
_____
_____
_____
_____
_____
_____

Conversations with my daughter have improved in these ways:

Date:___ / ___ / ___ _____

_____
_____
_____
_____
_____
_____
_____
_____
_____

Conversations with my daughter have improved in these ways:

Date:___/___/___ _____

_____

_____

_____

_____

_____

_____

_____

_____

_____

Conversations with my daughter have improved in these ways:

Date:___/___/___ _____

_____

_____

_____

_____

_____

_____

_____

_____

_____

_____

Conversations with my daughter have improved in these ways:

Date:___ /___ /___ _____

_____

_____

_____

_____

_____

_____

_____

_____

_____

Conversations with my daughter have improved in these ways:

Date:___ /___ /___ _____

_____

_____

_____

_____

_____

_____

_____

_____

_____

_____

CHAPTER TWO

○

Welcome to chapter 2 on our mission to help make sure your daughter feels LOVED. I hope you spent time reflecting and trying out your Listen exercises from Chapter One.

Let's review.

Listen to what is going on inside of you. Recognize what you are telling yourself. Are these positive or negative thoughts? Be mindful of the emotions they create and their potential impact. Choose to quiet yourself by putting your thoughts and feelings on a shelf, so you can truly listen to your daughter.

Okay, next we are focusing on the **O** in LOVED.

O is for **observe.**

Observe your daughter's body language. It is amazing how much information her body will communicate to you if you just look for it. This is great news, Mom. Free info!

When you are in conversation, observe her face. Is she flushed with anger? Are her eyebrows furrowed with anxiety? Is she looking you straight in the eye with confidence or is she trying to keep you from seeing the tears swelling? Is her body quiet, or are her arms flailing around?

It is now with your quieted mind (by listening to yourself from lesson 1) that you can do a great job of focusing on both your daughter's words and her body language. Your daughter is searching for words to match up with the new emotions she is experiencing. As she wrestles to figure out what she is feeling, her body physically acts out the struggle. Be patient and quietly observe.

Exercise: Tune Into Your Daughter's Body Language

Take a moment, twice a day, to consciously observe your daughter from head to toe. Tune in to her. Is she fidgeting? Expressing impatience by rolling her eyes? Stomping? Folding her arms while sitting quietly tense? Is her face flushed?

Does she look teary? What is her body telling you on the outside about how she is feeling on the inside? Check to see if her body language is matching what she is saying.

Exercise: Communicate with Emojis

Together with your daughter make a poster that has different faces or emojis on them with the description of what each face is feeling. Keep it up on either your fridge or on a corkboard in your house. Choose either a special magnet or a colored post-it note to represent each of you and place your magnet on the appropriate emoji so the other can easily see how you're feeling. This is a simple way for each of you to pause, reflect, and communicate how you are feeling to each other.

Journaling

Consciously tuning in to your daughter's body language twice every day will help you form the habit of doing it all the time. This is a great tool for you to use always. Take time to journal your observations of each day in this section. For additional journaling pages go here for a free printable template: bit.ly/LOVED-Journals and put into a 3 ring binder.

Our Emojis Project Experience

Write about your experience working with your daughter on this project. What did you talk about? Any cherished moments you want to remember?

_____

_____

_____

_____

_____

_____

_____

_____

_____

_____

_____

_____

_____

_____

_____

_____

_____

_____

_____

Today my daughter's body language told me this:

Date:___ /___ /___ _____

_____

_____

_____

_____

_____

_____

_____

_____

_____

_____

Today my daughter's body language told me this:

Date:___ /___ /___ _____

_____

_____

_____

_____

_____

_____

_____

_____

_____

_____

_____

Today my daughter's body language told me this:

Date:___/___/___ _____

_____

_____

_____

_____

_____

_____

_____

_____

_____

_____

Today my daughter's body language told me this:

Date:___/___/___ _____

_____

_____

_____

_____

_____

_____

_____

_____

_____

_____

_____

Today my daughter's body language told me this:

Date:___ / ___ / ___ _____

_____

_____

_____

_____

_____

_____

_____

_____

_____

Today my daughter's body language told me this:

Date:___ / ___ / ___ _____

_____

_____

_____

_____

_____

_____

_____

_____

_____

Today my daughter's body language told me this:

Date:___ /___/___ _____

_____

_____

_____

_____

_____

_____

_____

_____

_____

_____

Today my daughter's body language told me this:

Date:___ /___/___ _____

_____

_____

_____

_____

_____

_____

_____

_____

_____

_____

Today my daughter's body language told me this:

Date:___/___/___ _____

_____

_____

_____

_____

_____

_____

_____

_____

_____

_____

Today my daughter's body language told me this:

Date:___/___/___ _____

_____

_____

_____

_____

_____

_____

_____

_____

_____

_____

_____

Today my daughter's body language told me this:

Date:___/___/___ _____

_____

_____

_____

_____

_____

_____

_____

_____

_____

_____

Today my daughter's body language told me this:

Date:___/___/___ _____

_____

_____

_____

_____

_____

_____

_____

_____

_____

_____

_____

Today my daughter's body language told me this:

Date:___ /___ /___ _____

_____
_____
_____
_____
_____
_____
_____
_____
_____
_____

Today my daughter's body language told me this:

Date:___ /___ /___ _____

_____
_____
_____
_____
_____
_____
_____
_____
_____
_____
_____
_____

Today my daughter's body language told me this:

Date:___ /___ /___ _____

_____

_____

_____

_____

_____

_____

_____

_____

_____

Today my daughter's body language told me this:

Date:___ /___ /___ _____

_____

_____

_____

_____

_____

_____

_____

_____

_____

_____

Today my daughter's body language told me this:

Date:___ / ___ / ___ _____

_____

_____

_____

_____

_____

_____

_____

_____

_____

Today my daughter's body language told me this:

Date:___ / ___ / ___ _____

_____

_____

_____

_____

_____

_____

_____

_____

_____

_____

Today my daughter's body language told me this:

Date:___/___/___ _____

_____

_____

_____

_____

_____

_____

_____

_____

_____

_____

Today my daughter's body language told me this:

Date:___/___/___ _____

_____

_____

_____

_____

_____

_____

_____

_____

_____

_____

Today my daughter's body language told me this:

Date:___ /___ /___ _____

_____

_____

_____

_____

_____

_____

_____

_____

_____

Today my daughter's body language told me this:

Date:___ /___ /___ _____

_____

_____

_____

_____

_____

_____

_____

_____

_____

_____

Today my daughter's body language told me this:

Date:___/___/___ _____

_____

_____

_____

_____

_____

_____

_____

_____

Today my daughter's body language told me this:

Date:___/___/___ _____

_____

_____

_____

_____

_____

_____

_____

_____

Today my daughter's body language told me this:

Date:___ / ___ / ___ _____

_____

_____

_____

_____

_____

_____

_____

_____

_____

_____

_____

Today my daughter's body language told me this:

Date:___ / ___ / ___ _____

_____

_____

_____

_____

_____

_____

_____

_____

_____

_____

_____

_____

Today my daughter's body language told me this:

Date:___ /___ /___ _____

_____

_____

_____

_____

_____

_____

_____

_____

_____

_____

Today my daughter's body language told me this:

Date:___ /___ /___ _____

_____

_____

_____

_____

_____

_____

_____

_____

_____

_____

_____

Today my daughter's body language told me this:

Date:___/___/___ _____

_____

_____

_____

_____

_____

_____

_____

_____

_____

_____

Today my daughter's body language told me this:

Date:___/___/___ _____

_____

_____

_____

_____

_____

_____

_____

_____

_____

_____

_____

_____

Today my daughter's body language told me this:

Date:___/___/___ _____

_____

_____

_____

_____

_____

_____

_____

_____

_____

Today my daughter's body language told me this:

Date:___/___/___ _____

_____

_____

_____

_____

_____

_____

_____

_____

_____

_____

Today my daughter's body language told me this:

Date:___ / ___ / ___ _____

_____

_____

_____

_____

_____

_____

_____

_____

_____

_____

Today my daughter's body language told me this:

Date:___ / ___ / ___ _____

_____

_____

_____

_____

_____

_____

_____

_____

_____

_____

_____

Today my daughter's body language told me this:

Date:___ /___ /___ _____

_____

_____

_____

_____

_____

_____

_____

_____

_____

_____

Today my daughter's body language told me this:

Date:___ /___ /___ _____

_____

_____

_____

_____

_____

_____

_____

_____

_____

_____

CHAPTER THREE

V

Welcome to Chapter Three on our mission to make sure your daughter feels LOVED. So far we have learned about the L and the O in LOVED.

Let's review.

Listen to what is going on inside of your head. Recognize what you are telling yourself. Are these positive or negative thoughts? Be mindful of the emotions they create and their potential impact. Choose to quiet yourself by putting your thoughts and feelings on a shelf, so you can truly listen to your daughter.

Observe your daughter's body language. Look for the clues that tell you what is going on inside.

Now we are focusing on the letter **V** in the word LOVED.

V is for **validate.**

Validate your daughter's feelings by giving her your undivided attention. That means stop what you are doing, make eye contact, keep your body quiet, listen intently, and fully engage your compassionate heart. If that is not possible, let her know you want to give her your full attention but that you can't right at that moment. Make a plan for when you can.

Decide this together. In doing so, you reaffirm that her feelings matter. You also communicate that you want to be there for her.

With your quieted mind you will be a good listener. You will be able to observe some of her feelings that have not found words yet. By making sure you can fully listen to her, you will be validating her emotions.

These are powerful tools for strengthening your bond with your daughter!

Exercise: Focused, Heart-to-Heart Conversations

Today when your daughter starts talking to you, stop what you are doing, and look into her eyes. Surprise her with your full attention.

If you are driving, and you have the time, take a moment to pull over. If she asks why you stopped, respond, "I want to focus on what you have to say." This is a great way to reaffirm that she matters.

If you can't pull over tell her, "I am looking forward to giving you my full attention as soon as we get home. Driving distracts me from hearing all you have to share, and I want to hear everything!" Doing this is another way you can communicate, "I love you!"

Exercise: Handmade Love Notes

Sharing words of support after a heartfelt conversation is something your daughter will never outgrow. Create a homemade card. This does not need to be extravagant. Something as simple as a piece of paper folded in half with a heart drawn on it will connect with your daughter's heart. If you sometimes have trouble finding your words, here are a few phrases to help you get your juices flowing:

- Sweetie, thank you for sharing your feelings with me today.
- Thank you for helping me understand why today was so upsetting to you.
- You are so brave. Thank you for sharing your heart with me today.
- I am so sorry you had a difficult day. I know you will get through this.
- I am here to support you, Honey.
- I am so proud of who you are and who you are becoming.
- Always remember, no matter what, I love you.

Write your phrases here.

_____

_____

_____

_____

_____

Heart-to-Heart Conversation Review

Reflect and write about your conversation with your daughter. Did it go as planned? Maybe you have a few kinks to work out. Also, write about your love notes experience after you give them to her.

_____

_____

_____

_____

_____

_____

_____

_____

_____

_____

_____

_____

_____

_____

_____

_____

_____

_____

Journaling

Reflect daily and write about moments you have validated your daughter, and how she responded. For additional pages go here for a free printable template: bit.ly/LOVED-Journals and put into a 3 ring binder.

How I validated my daughter and how she responded:

Date:___/___/___ _____

_____

_____

_____

_____

_____

_____

_____

_____

_____

_____

How I validated my daughter and how she responded:

Date:___/___/___ _____

_____

_____

_____

_____

_____

_____

_____

_____

_____

_____

_____

How I validated my daughter and how she responded:

Date:___/___/___ _____

_____

_____

_____

_____

_____

_____

_____

_____

_____

How I validated my daughter and how she responded:

Date:___/___/___ _____

_____

_____

_____

_____

_____

_____

_____

_____

_____

_____

How I validated my daughter and how she responded:

Date:___/___/___ _____

_____

_____

_____

_____

_____

_____

_____

_____

_____

_____

How I validated my daughter and how she responded:

Date:___/___/___ _____

_____

_____

_____

_____

_____

_____

_____

_____

_____

_____

_____

How I validated my daughter and how she responded:

Date:___ /___ /___ _____

_____

_____

_____

_____

_____

_____

_____

_____

_____

How I validated my daughter and how she responded:

Date:___ /___ /___ _____

_____

_____

_____

_____

_____

_____

_____

_____

_____

_____

How I validated my daughter and how she responded:

Date:___/___/___ _____

_____

_____

_____

_____

_____

_____

_____

_____

_____

_____

How I validated my daughter and how she responded:

Date:___/___/___ _____

_____

_____

_____

_____

_____

_____

_____

_____

_____

_____

_____

How I validated my daughter and how she responded:

Date:___ / ___ / ___ _____

_____

_____

_____

_____

_____

_____

_____

_____

_____

_____

_____

How I validated my daughter and how she responded:

Date:___ / ___ / ___ _____

_____

_____

_____

_____

_____

_____

_____

_____

_____

_____

_____

_____

How I validated my daughter and how she responded:

Date:___/___/___ _____

_____

_____

_____

_____

_____

_____

_____

_____

_____

_____

How I validated my daughter and how she responded:

Date:___/___/___ _____

_____

_____

_____

_____

_____

_____

_____

_____

_____

_____

_____

How I validated my daughter and how she responded:

Date:___/___/___ _____

_____

_____

_____

_____

_____

_____

_____

_____

_____

How I validated my daughter and how she responded:

Date:___/___/___ _____

_____

_____

_____

_____

_____

_____

_____

_____

_____

_____

How I validated my daughter and how she responded:

Date:___ / ___ / ___ _____
_____
_____
_____
_____
_____
_____
_____
_____
_____
_____

How I validated my daughter and how she responded:

Date:___ / ___ / ___ _____
_____
_____
_____
_____
_____
_____
_____
_____
_____
_____

How I validated my daughter and how she responded:

Date:___/___/___ _____

_____
_____
_____
_____
_____
_____
_____
_____
_____

How I validated my daughter and how she responded:

Date:___/___/___ _____

_____
_____
_____
_____
_____
_____
_____
_____
_____
_____

How I validated my daughter and how she responded:

Date:___/___/___ _____
_____
_____
_____
_____
_____
_____
_____
_____
_____
_____

How I validated my daughter and how she responded:

Date:___/___/___ _____
_____
_____
_____
_____
_____
_____
_____
_____
_____
_____
_____

How I validated my daughter and how she responded:

Date:___ /___ /___ _____

_____

_____

_____

_____

_____

_____

_____

_____

_____

_____

How I validated my daughter and how she responded:

Date:___ /___ /___ _____

_____

_____

_____

_____

_____

_____

_____

_____

_____

_____

_____

How I validated my daughter and how she responded:

Date:___/___/___ _____

_____

_____

_____

_____

_____

_____

_____

_____

_____

_____

How I validated my daughter and how she responded:

Date:___/___/___ _____

_____

_____

_____

_____

_____

_____

_____

_____

_____

_____

_____

How I validated my daughter and how she responded:

Date:___ /___ /___ _____

_____
_____
_____
_____
_____
_____
_____
_____
_____
_____

How I validated my daughter and how she responded:

Date:___ /___ /___ _____

_____
_____
_____
_____
_____
_____
_____
_____
_____
_____

How I validated my daughter and how she responded:

Date:___ / ___ / ___ _____
_____
_____
_____
_____
_____
_____
_____
_____
_____
_____

How I validated my daughter and how she responded:

Date:___ / ___ / ___ _____
_____
_____
_____
_____
_____
_____
_____
_____
_____
_____

How I validated my daughter and how she responded:

Date:___/___/___ _____

_____

_____

_____

_____

_____

_____

_____

_____

_____

_____

How I validated my daughter and how she responded:

Date:___/___/___ _____

_____

_____

_____

_____

_____

_____

_____

_____

_____

_____

_____

How I validated my daughter and how she responded:

Date:___ / ___ / ___ _____

_____

_____

_____

_____

_____

_____

_____

_____

_____

How I validated my daughter and how she responded:

Date:___ / ___ / ___ _____

_____

_____

_____

_____

_____

_____

_____

_____

_____

_____

How I validated my daughter and how she responded:

Date:___/___/___ _____

_____

_____

_____

_____

_____

_____

_____

_____

_____

_____

How I validated my daughter and how she responded:

Date:___/___/___ _____

_____

_____

_____

_____

_____

_____

_____

_____

_____

_____

_____

CHAPTER FOUR

E

Welcome to Chapter Four on our mission to make sure your daughter feels LOVED. So far we have learned about the letters L-O-V in LOVED.

Let's review.

Listen to what is going on inside of your head. Recognize what you are telling yourself. Are these positive or negative thoughts? Be mindful of the emotions they create and their potential impact. Choose to quiet yourself down by putting your thoughts and feelings on a shelf, so you can truly listen to your daughter.

Observe your daughter's body language. Look for the clues that tell you what is going on inside.

Validate your daughter's feelings by making sure you are giving her your full attention, with eye contact, focused listening, quiet body, and a compassionate heart.

Next, we are focusing on the letter **E** in the word LOVED.

E is for **encourage.**

Encourage your daughter to share her feelings. Remember, she is experiencing emotions she has never felt before. It is scary to be confronted with feelings that are unfamiliar. She will struggle to find words to express herself. Be patient. Don't interrupt or put words in her mouth. Stay calm. Doing this will help her feel safe, relaxed, and more willing to be open with you.

Words of affirmation will help build her confidence, so encourage her by pointing out her strengths. Celebrate her effort. Communicate that persistently doing her best will become her superpower in life.

By choosing to listen, observe, validate, and encourage your daughter, you are strongly communicating, "I am here for you. I care about your feelings and what you are experiencing."

Exercise: Cheers!

Cheers! is a fun activity you can do together that will provide you with insight into what affirmations most deeply touch her heart.

One way to encourage your daughter is by becoming her cheerleader. Set aside some one-on-one time with your daughter to work on this project together.

INGREDIENTS

- 1 large piece of white construction paper
- 1 pack of crayons, pens, or colored pencils (or all of these things if you like)
- Warm, happy ambiance

STEPS

1. Have your daughter draw a picture of you as her cheerleader. Have her draw you yelling into a megaphone while standing on a platform.

2. On the outside of the megaphone have her write down different phrases that would make her feel supported and cheered on.

3. Then around the platform have her write down all the things that you could do to make her feel supported and lifted up.

4. Talk through the different words of cheer she has listed. Encourage her to tell you more about these certain words and phrases. Ask her, "How would hearing these words make you feel?"

5. Together, come up with specific things you could do to make your daughter feel even more supported by you.

Our Cheers Exercise Experience

What have you learned about your daughter while working on this project? Write down your favorite moments from this experience together.

_____

_____

_____

_____

_____

_____

_____

_____

_____

_____

_____

_____

_____

_____

_____

_____

_____

_____

_____

_____

_____

_____

Exercise: Give Her Compliments

Look for opportunities to affirm your daughter. Point out what she does well. Compliment her for doing her best. Say, "Good job!" "Thank you. That was helpful." or "I am proud of you for trying so hard!" See how she responds. Does she look surprised? Does she stand up straighter? Give her a reason to feel good about herself. This will help her feel safe and to be more open with you.

Journaling

Write what you complimented your daughter on and how she responded. This may help you see what affirmations connect with her best. For additional journaling pages go here for a free printable template: bit.ly/LOVED-Journals and put into a 3-ring binder.

Complimenting my beautiful girl and how she responded:

Date:___ / ___ / ___ _____

_____

_____

_____

_____

_____

_____

_____

_____

_____

_____

Complimenting my beautiful girl and how she responded:

Date:___ / ___ / ___ _____

_____

_____

_____

_____

_____

_____

_____

_____

_____

_____

_____

Complimenting my beautiful girl and how she responded:

Date:___ / ___ / ___ _____

_____

_____

_____

_____

_____

_____

_____

_____

_____

_____

Complimenting my beautiful girl and how she responded:

Date:___ / ___ / ___ _____

_____

_____

_____

_____

_____

_____

_____

_____

_____

_____

_____

Complimenting my beautiful girl and how she responded:

Date:___ /___ /___ _____

_____

_____

_____

_____

_____

_____

_____

_____

_____

_____

Complimenting my beautiful girl and how she responded:

Date:___ /___ /___ _____

_____

_____

_____

_____

_____

_____

_____

_____

_____

_____

_____

Complimenting my beautiful girl and how she responded:

Date:___/___/___ _____

_____

_____

_____

_____

_____

_____

_____

_____

_____

_____

Complimenting my beautiful girl and how she responded:

Date:___/___/___ _____

_____

_____

_____

_____

_____

_____

_____

_____

_____

_____

Complimenting my beautiful girl and how she responded:

Date:___ /___/___ _____

_____

_____

_____

_____

_____

_____

_____

_____

_____

_____

Complimenting my beautiful girl and how she responded:

Date:___ /___/___ _____

_____

_____

_____

_____

_____

_____

_____

_____

_____

_____

_____

Complimenting my beautiful girl and how she responded:

Date:___ / ___ / ___ _____

_____

_____

_____

_____

_____

_____

_____

_____

_____

_____

Complimenting my beautiful girl and how she responded:

Date:___ / ___ / ___ _____

_____

_____

_____

_____

_____

_____

_____

_____

_____

_____

_____

Complimenting my beautiful girl and how she responded:

Date:___/___/___ _____

_____

_____

_____

_____

_____

_____

_____

_____

_____

Complimenting my beautiful girl and how she responded:

Date:___/___/___ _____

_____

_____

_____

_____

_____

_____

_____

_____

_____

_____

Complimenting my beautiful girl and how she responded:

Date:___ / ___ / ___ _____

_____

_____

_____

_____

_____

_____

_____

_____

_____

_____

Complimenting my beautiful girl and how she responded:

Date:___ / ___ / ___ _____

_____

_____

_____

_____

_____

_____

_____

_____

_____

_____

_____

Complimenting my beautiful girl and how she responded:

Date:___/___/___ _____

_____

_____

_____

_____

_____

_____

_____

_____

_____

Complimenting my beautiful girl and how she responded:

Date:___/___/___ _____

_____

_____

_____

_____

_____

_____

_____

_____

_____

_____

Complimenting my beautiful girl and how she responded:

Date:___ /___ /___ _____

_____

_____

_____

_____

_____

_____

_____

_____

_____

_____

Complimenting my beautiful girl and how she responded:

Date:___ /___ /___ _____

_____

_____

_____

_____

_____

_____

_____

_____

_____

_____

_____

Complimenting my beautiful girl and how she responded:

Date:___ /___ /___ _____

_____

_____

_____

_____

_____

_____

_____

_____

_____

_____

Complimenting my beautiful girl and how she responded:

Date:___ /___ /___ _____

_____

_____

_____

_____

_____

_____

_____

_____

_____

_____

_____

Complimenting my beautiful girl and how she responded:

Date:___ / ___ / ___ _____

_____

_____

_____

_____

_____

_____

_____

_____

_____

Complimenting my beautiful girl and how she responded:

Date:___ / ___ / ___ _____

_____

_____

_____

_____

_____

_____

_____

_____

_____

Complimenting my beautiful girl and how she responded:

Date:___/___/___ _____

_____

_____

_____

_____

_____

_____

_____

_____

_____

_____

Complimenting my beautiful girl and how she responded:

Date:___/___/___ _____

_____

_____

_____

_____

_____

_____

_____

_____

_____

_____

_____

Complimenting my beautiful girl and how she responded:

Date:___/___/___ _____

_____

_____

_____

_____

_____

_____

_____

_____

_____

_____

Complimenting my beautiful girl and how she responded:

Date:___/___/___ _____

_____

_____

_____

_____

_____

_____

_____

_____

_____

_____

Complimenting my beautiful girl and how she responded:

Date:___ / ___ / ___ _____

_____

_____

_____

_____

_____

_____

_____

_____

_____

_____

Complimenting my beautiful girl and how she responded:

Date:___ / ___ / ___ _____

_____

_____

_____

_____

_____

_____

_____

_____

_____

_____

_____

Complimenting my beautiful girl and how she responded:

Date:___ /___ /___ _____

_____

_____

_____

_____

_____

_____

_____

_____

_____

_____

Complimenting my beautiful girl and how she responded:

Date:___ /___ /___ _____

_____

_____

_____

_____

_____

_____

_____

_____

_____

_____

_____

Complimenting my beautiful girl and how she responded:

Date:___ / ___ / ___ _____

_____

_____

_____

_____

_____

_____

_____

_____

_____

_____

Complimenting my beautiful girl and how she responded:

Date:___ / ___ / ___ _____

_____

_____

_____

_____

_____

_____

_____

_____

_____

_____

_____

_____

Complimenting my beautiful girl and how she responded:

Date:___/___/___ _____

_____

_____

_____

_____

_____

_____

_____

_____

_____

Complimenting my beautiful girl and how she responded:

Date:___/___/___ _____

_____

_____

_____

_____

_____

_____

_____

_____

_____

_____

Complimenting my beautiful girl and how she responded:

Date:___/___/___ _____

_____

_____

_____

_____

_____

_____

_____

_____

_____

_____

Complimenting my beautiful girl and how she responded:

Date:___/___/___ _____

_____

_____

_____

_____

_____

_____

_____

_____

_____

_____

_____

CHAPTER FIVE

Yay, Mom! You have made it to Chapter Five! This is our final session on our mission to make sure your daughter feels LOVED.

Look at what you have learned: the letters L-O-V-E in LOVED. Let's review.

Listen to what is going on inside of your head. Recognize what you are telling yourself. Are these positive or negative thoughts? Be mindful of the emotions they create and their potential impact. Choose to quiet yourself by putting your thoughts and feelings on a shelf. Now you can truly listen to your daughter.

Observe your daughter's body language. Look for the clues that tell you what is going on inside.

Validate your daughter's feelings by making sure you are giving her your full attention, with eye contact, focused listening, quiet body, and a compassionate heart.

Encourage your daughter to share with you her thoughts and feelings free of judgment. Encouraging words of affirmation about what she does well and affirming her efforts builds her confidence and desire to be persistent. It also helps create a place that will make her feel safe enough to open up and share her feelings.

Finally, we are focusing on the letter **D** in the word LOVED. **D** is for **discover**.

Discover your own hot buttons. (*No, Janet, don't make me!*) You know what? You have already been wrestling with your hot buttons subconsciously, so why not just face them?

Because, believe it or not, when you know what your hot buttons are, they can empower you. They can help you find something your daughter truly needs—empathy. Many of your hot buttons were caused by an experience you had during our own teenage years. When you spend time remembering your own painful moments, you will be more understanding of your daughter's feelings.

Recognizing your hot buttons makes you self-aware. This awareness gives you the power to choose how you want to respond to a situation instead of spontaneously overreacting. You get to choose to keep calm because you are conscious of their existence.

Your daughter, without knowing it, has been pushing your buttons regularly. She struggles with uncertainty, friendships gone wrong, and a broken heart. Her emotions stir up your own memories, whether you realize it or not.

When you are not consciously aware of your own hot buttons, you will accidentally overreact when they are pushed. This will bring more pain and conflict to your mother-daughter relationship. Facing your own pain can help you understand it, get through it, and separate it from your daughter's pain. Turn your pain into your power.

So, discovering your hot buttons is ultimately a very good thing!

Exercise: Write in Your Journal

Journaling is a powerful tool that equips you to better manage your mind-set and social interactions with others. This will make a huge difference in helping you discover what is going on inside of you. It is also kind of like taking yourself on a date. Of all the people in the world, the most important person listening to your feelings is you!

This assignment will be a two-stage experience. Once every morning, you will write in The Morning Purge pages, and once every night, you will write in My Thank-You pages.

Go to bit.ly/LOVED-Journals for a free template for these pages and create your journal sections. Create a section in your three-ring binder for these entries.

Journaling Part 1: The Morning Purge

Get up 15–30 minutes earlier than usual. This journaling will help you record your first feelings of the day. Often when we first wake up, we have a bunch of negative gobbledygook that clogs up our ability to embrace a new day. The morning purge gives you a chance to off-load those icky things, so you can think more clearly.

To the right of the page you will find space to write down those random to-dos that pop into your head. At the end of your journaling session, write down one positive thought under Today's Positivity.

After eight weeks, set aside some alone time to go back and read through your Morning Purges. Use two different-colored pens to highlight (1) insights and (2) actions needed. Ask yourself these questions:

- Who have I been continuing to complain about?
- What have I been procrastinating?
- What things have I grown to accept?
- What things have I changed?

You may notice your writing has been very black and white. This is normal. No worries. These pages have allowed you to acknowledge your feelings. Becoming conscious of them makes it easier for you to be aware of your emotions throughout the day. This gives you more control over them as you interact with your daughter and your family.

This is a very good thing!

Take what you have learned about yourself and use this information. Act on what you have learned. If you experienced progress and gained a deeper understanding of yourself and your daughter, consider doing it again for another eight weeks.

Journaling Part 2: My Thank-You Pages

In the evening before bed, set aside 5–15 minutes to write down all the things you are thankful for. Include accomplishments that made you proud of yourself, nice things that happened, or a kindness done for you by others.

The likelihood that *at least one good thing happened* during the day is very high. It is worth searching for. As you write down each positive thing, take a moment to focus on it. Remember the details of what happened and what or who made it so positive. Let your body reexperience the moment. Doing so automatically causes your brain to create serotonin, a chemical that makes you feel good and helps you quickly relax. This will not only be good for your heart and soul but will also help you prepare for sleep.

Mom, if you have not written in a single journal while reading this book, this is the journal to commit to. Because this will be the journal you add to, as well as reflect on, *for the rest of your life.* Your own words will deliver encouragement and inspiration to you.

Also, it doesn't matter whether you use the pages we've provided, buy yourself a special leather diary, type up your happy memories, paint them across your ceiling, turn them into songs, or speak your thoughts into a voice app on your phone.

It doesn't matter *how* you do it. It matters *that* you do it. This is the current you giving a priceless heirloom to the future you.

Your *Thank-You Pages* will lift your spirits on difficult days. They'll remind you that *you are becoming the mom you want to be.* They'll nurture an ever-deepening attitude of gratitude within your heart. And in doing so, you will be encouraged and feel empowered to take on the world, whatever the day brings!

If you choose to use the journaling pages we've provided, go here for a free printable template: bit.ly/LOVED-Journals.

CHAPTER SIX

Hooray!

Celebrate all that you have learned . . . so that your daughter feels LOVED!

Put aside some time to really do something special for yourself. Make a little purchase just for you, have coffee with a friend, or take a bubble bath. Whatever you do, remember it is important to celebrate your accomplishments. You deserve it!

What a powerful package you now have inside the word LOVED.

Listening to yourself and quieting your mind, together, unlock the door to making sure your daughter feels loved. Now you can **listen** to your daughter's words while **observing** her body language. You will **validate** her feelings with your full attention and **encourage** her to share free of judgment. Finally, she will mirror the empathy you **discovered** behind your own emotional hot buttons.

You are doing an excellent job of taking care of yourself, your daughter, and your relationship with each other. Reread this book to refresh your memory on all that you have learned. Keep writing and refer to your journal when you feel discouraged, and gain hope in the progress you have made.

With all my heart I cheer you! You are on your way to making sure your daughter feels LOVED!

Mom . . . *keep calm and listen on.*

Mama Bear, thank you for reading *L.O.V.E.D.* It means so much to me!

Keep the love and support flowing in your life. Join our *Mom Keep Calm* tribe and continue equipping yourself with relational tools to keep you going and growing! Be the first to hear about new programs to support your mission to be an empowered, confident, and happy mom. Receive just the right amount of emails (not too many, not too few) to keep you in the loop of what *Mom Keep Calm* is cooking up for you, without clogging up your inbox.

To join the *Mom Keep Calm* tribe, go to: www.momkeepcalm. com/3-secrets/. Continue getting the love and support you deserve!

One more thing. Please help spread the calm! If you have five minutes, you'd make this Mama Bear very happy if you could write a short Amazon review. Your words will motivate Amazon to get the word out about *L.O.V.E.D.* And then this powerful book will help more moms raising teen girls, all around the world.

Mom! Stay tuned for *L.O.V.E.D. Daughter's Edition* coming out soon.

L.O.V.E.D. Daughter's Edition will help your daughter grow more confident in herself and her ability to communicate clearly with you and others. It will provide her with tools to help her avoid feeling overwhelmed and equip her with skills to better understand her own feelings.

Because when your daughter understands herself, she will feel less anxious. The noise of her worries will quiet down. She will feel more centered. Your little lady will be able to hear you again and your messages of love will touch her heart.

Be in the know! Now you can be the first to hear about the launch of *L.O.V.E.D. Daughter's Edition.*

It's easy. Click this link and join our tribe today! www.momkeepcalm.com/3-secrets/

ABOUT THE AUTHOR

Janet Lund is a youth minister with many years of experience working with teenagers, including her own daughter. She lives in Boise, Idaho, where she enjoys the company of her husband, daughter, and pets.

www.MomKeepCalm.com

M♥M Keep Calm

www.ingramcontent.com/pod-product-compliance
Lightning Source LLC
Chambersburg PA
CBHW072040040426
42447CB00012BB/2947